RUTH AND ESTHER

A Bible Reader

Ruth and Esther
A Bible Reader

Second Adam Publishing edition 2013
www.secondadampublishing.com

All scripture quotations, unless otherwise indicated, are taken from the *The World English Bible* (WEB). The WEB is a public domain modern english translation of the Holy Bible, based on the American Standard Version of the Holy Bible first published in 1901, the Biblia Hebraica Stutgartensa Old Testament, and the Greek Majority Text New Testament. The OT version used in this book was in a draft form at the time of publication.

Pictures used with permission: © 2006 www.TheGloryStory.com

Printed in the United States
ISBN: 978-0615779423

ESTHER AND RUTH
A Bible Reader

Second Adam Publishing

CONTENTS

Dedicated to
Our Lord and Savior Jesus Christ
My wife and our two girls:
Katie and Savannah

PREFACE
(For Parents)

"These words, which I command you this day, shall be on your heart; and you shall *teach them diligently to your children*, and shall talk of them when you sit in your house, and when you walk by the way, and when you lie down, and when you rise up."

Deuteronomy 6: 6-7 (emphasis added)

O ur perspective of life is very limited. We tend to view it in number of years; ninety years is seen as a good long life. Life nonetheless is eternal. The question is where you will spend it; heaven or hell. We can know the answer to this question simply by studying the word of God.

Parents, one aspect of our limited perspective of life does have some usefulness, that is, its limitedness. This limitedness of life can be no more appreciated than in seeing how quickly our children grow. It is during their youth that we have the greatest influence on them. We know from scripture that those who meditate on God's word are like trees that grow along the streams. They grow tall and healthy with roots down deep. This is why God has placed so much importance on teaching our children early the need to understand God's word; so much, that He has commanded you to *teach them diligently.*

INTRODUCTION
(For Children)

T hese Bible stories are more than just stories. They are real! They are about real places, real people, and a real God. They were written by God through real men. Just like you use your pencil in school to write a story, God used people. God gave these stories to us for an important reason; so we can know Him and what He expects of us. If you do not read the Bible you can never know who the true God is.

The Book of Ruth

The story of Ruth takes places when judges still ruled Israel and they did not have a king. Most likely this took place when Jair was Judge (Judges 10:3-5) approximately between 1126 to 1105 B.C. Ruth is a Moabite who married into a Jewish family. After her husband dies, she travels with her mother-in-law to Bethlehem to start a new life. Her trust in God and her obedience to her mother-in-law is used by God to bring about His plan for Israel.

The Book of Esther

Esther takes place in the country of Persia where the Jewish people have been exiled and are waiting for God to bring them home. Some had already started this journey years earlier but the rest still remain. By God's design, Esther becomes Queen of Persia during the rule of King Ahasuerus (uh-has'yoo-er´uhs) sometime around 479 B.C. and is used by God to help protect the Jewish people.

Throughout this book you will notice that God's name is called 'Yahweh." In many Bibles this word is translated into "the LORD." Yahweh is the Jewish word for God.

I hope that when you read these stories that you learn more about God and how He wants you to be.

Enjoy!

Chapter One

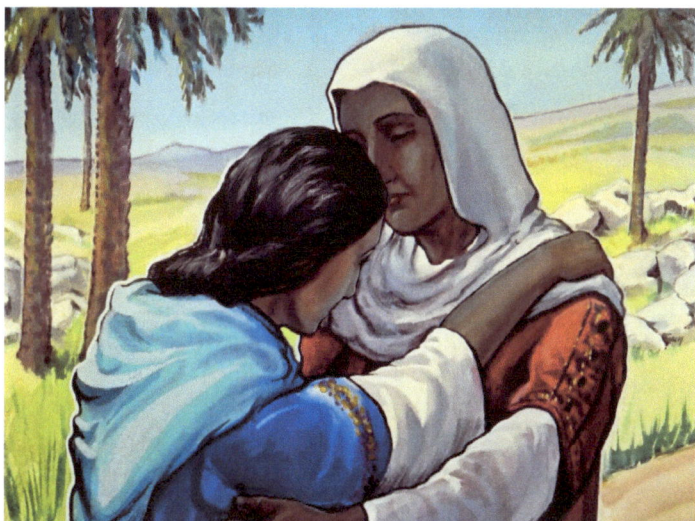

1 It happened in the days when the judges judged, that there was a famine in the land. A certain man of Bethlehem-judah went to sojourn in the country of Moab, he, and his wife, and his two sons. **2** The name of the man was Elimelech, and the name of his wife Naomi, and the name of his two sons Mahlon and Chilion, Ephrathites of Bethlehem-judah. They came into the country of Moab, and continued there. **3** Elimelech, Naomi's husband, died; and she was left, and her two sons. **4** They took them wives of the women of Moab; the name of the one was Orpah, and the name of the other Ruth: and they lived there about ten years. **5** Mahlon and Chilion died both of them; and the woman was left of her two children and of her husband. **6** Then she arose with her daughters-in-law, that she might return from the country of Moab: for she had heard in the country of Moab how that Yahweh had visited his people in giving them bread. **7** She went forth out of the place where she was, and her two daughters-in-law with her; and they went on the way to return to the land of Judah. **8** Naomi said to her two daughters-in-law, Go, return each of you to her mother's house: Yahweh deal kindly with you, as you have dealt with the dead, and with me. **9** Yahweh grant you that you may find rest, each of you in the house of her husband. Then she kissed them, and they lifted up their voice, and wept. **10** They said to her, No, but we will return with you to your people. **11** Naomi said, Turn again, my daughters: why will you go with me? have I yet sons in my womb, that they may be your husbands? **12** Turn again, my daughters, go your way; for I am too old to have a husband. If I should say, I have hope, if I should even have a husband tonight, and should also bear sons; **13** would you therefore wait until they were grown? would you therefore stay from having husbands? nay, my daughters, for it grieves me much for your sakes, for the hand of Yahweh is gone forth against me. **14** They lifted up their voice, and wept again: and Orpah kissed her mother-in-law, but Ruth joined with her. **15** She said, Behold, your sister-in-law is gone back to her people, and to her god: return you after your sister-in-law. **16** Ruth said, "Don't entreat me to leave you, and to return from following after you, for where you go, I will go; and where you lodge, I will lodge; your people shall be my people, and your God my God; **17** where you die, will I die, and there will I be buried: Yahweh do so to me, and more also, if anything but death part you and me." **18** When she saw that she was steadfastly minded to go with her, she left off speaking to her. **19** So they two went until they came to Bethlehem. It happened, when they were come to Bethlehem, that all the city was moved about them, and [the women] said, Is this Naomi? **20** She said to them, "Don't call me Naomi, call me Mara; for the Almighty has dealt very bitterly with me. **21** I went out full, and Yahweh has brought me home again empty; why do you call me Naomi, seeing Yahweh has testified against me, and the Almighty has afflicted me?" **22** So Naomi returned, and Ruth the Moabitess, her daughter-in-law, with her, who returned out of the country of Moab: and they came to Bethlehem in the beginning of barley harvest.

Did you know?

When reaching Israel, Naomi was greeted by her old friends, however she was very upset because of what had happen to her husband and sons. She asked that they call her by a new name. But what does this mean? Naomi's name means something in her native language. Her name means "pleasant". When returning home she asked to be called Mara, which means "bitter". Why do you think she wanted to be called bitter? Do you think God was happy with her attitude? What blessing does Naomi have that she should be thankful for?

Chapter Two

1 Naomi had a kinsman of her husband's, a mighty man of wealth, of the family of Elimelech, and his name was Boaz. **2** Ruth the Moabitess said to Naomi, Let me now go to the field, and glean among the ears of grain after him in whose sight I shall find favor. She said to her, Go, my daughter. **3** She went, and came and gleaned in the field after the reapers: and she happened to come to the portion of the field belonging to Boaz, who was of the family of Elimelech. **4** Behold, Boaz came from Bethlehem, and said to the reapers, Yahweh be with you. They answered him, Yahweh bless you. **5** Then said Boaz to his servant who was set over the reapers, Whose young lady is this? **6** The servant who was set over the reapers answered, It is the Moabite lady who came back with Naomi out of the country of Moab: **7** She said, Please let me glean and gather after the reapers among the sheaves. So she came, and has continued even from the morning until now, except that she stayed a little in the house. **8** Then said Boaz to Ruth, Don't you hear, my daughter? Don't go to glean in another field, neither pass from hence, but abide here fast by my maidens. **9** Let your eyes be on the field that they reap, and go after them: haven't I charged the young men that they shall not touch you? and when you are thirsty, go to the vessels, and drink of that which the young men have drawn. **10** Then she fell on her face, and bowed herself to the ground, and said to him, Why have I found favor in your sight, that you should take knowledge of me, seeing I am a foreigner? **11** Boaz answered her, It has fully been shown me, all that you have done to your mother-in-law since the death of your husband; and how you have left your father and your mother, and the land of your birth, and have come to a people that you didn't know before. **12** Yahweh recompense your work, and a full reward be given you of Yahweh, the God of Israel, under whose wings you are come to take refuge. **13** Then she said, Let me find favor in your sight, my lord, because you have comforted me, and because you have spoken kindly to your handmaid, though I am not as one of your handmaidens. **14** At meal-time Boaz said to her, Come here, and eat of the bread, and dip your morsel in the vinegar. She sat beside the reapers, and they reached her parched grain, and she ate, and was sufficed, and left of it. **15** When she was risen up to glean, Boaz commanded his young men, saying, Let her glean even among the sheaves, and don't reproach her. **16** Also pull out some for her from the bundles, and leave it, and let her glean, and don't rebuke her. **17** So she gleaned in the field until evening; and she beat out that which she had gleaned, and it was about an ephah of barley. **18** She took it up, and went into the city; and her mother-in-law saw what she had gleaned: and she brought forth and gave to her that which she had left after she was sufficed. **19** Her mother-in-law said to her, Where have you gleaned today? and where have you worked? blessed be he who did take knowledge of you. She shown her mother-in-law with whom she had worked, and said, The man's name with whom I worked today is Boaz. **20** Naomi said to her daughter-in-law, Blessed be he of Yahweh, who has not left off his kindness to the living and to the dead. Naomi said to her, The man is a close relative to us, one of our near kinsmen. **21** Ruth the Moabitess said, Yes, he said to me, You shall keep fast by my young men, until they have ended all my harvest. **22** Naomi said to Ruth her daughter-in-law, It is good, my daughter, that you go out with his maidens, and that they not meet you in any other field. **23** So she kept fast by the maidens of Boaz, to glean to the end of barley harvest and of wheat harvest; and she lived with her mother-in-law.

Did you know?

The Law of Moses made a provision for the needy and widows. (A widow is a woman whose husband has died) In Leviticus 23:22 it says, "When you reap the harvest of your land, you shall not wholly reap the corners of your field, neither shall you gather the gleaning of your harvest: you shall leave them for the poor, and for the sojourner: I am Yahweh your God."

Do you see how God has provided for Naomi and Ruth? Do you see how God has also lead Ruth to the field of Boaz instead of someone else?

This is an example of how God has already arranged certain events to fulfill his plan. We call this God's providence. Have you noticed God's providence in your own life?

Chapter Three

1 Naomi her mother-in-law said to her, My daughter, shall I not seek rest for you, that it may be well with you? **2** Now isn't Boaz our kinsman, with whose maidens you were? Behold, he winnows barley tonight in the threshing floor. **3** Wash yourself therefore, and anoint you, and put your clothing on you, and get you down to the threshing floor, but don't make yourself known to the man, until he shall have done eating and drinking. **4** It shall be, when he lies down, that you shall mark the place where he shall lie, and you shall go in, and uncover his feet, and lay you down; and he will tell you what you shall do. **5** She said to her,

All that you say I will do. **6** She went down to the threshing floor, and did according to all that her mother-in-law bade her. **7** When Boaz had eaten and drunk, and his heart was merry, he went to lie down at the end of the heap of grain: and she came softly, and uncovered his feet, and laid her down. **8** It happened at midnight, that the man was afraid, and turned himself; and, behold, a woman lay at his feet. **9** He said, Who are you? She answered, I am Ruth your handmaid: spread therefore your skirt over your handmaid; for you are a near kinsman. **10** He said, Blessed are you by Yahweh, my daughter: you have shown more kindness in the latter end than at the beginning, inasmuch as you didn't follow young men, whether poor or rich. **11** Now, my daughter, don't be afraid; I will do to you all that you say; for all the city of my people does know that you are a worthy woman. **12** Now it is true that I am a near kinsman; however there is a kinsman nearer than I. **13** Stay this night, and it shall be in the morning, that if he will perform to you the part of a kinsman, well; let him do the kinsman's part: but if he will not do the part of a kinsman to you, then will I do the part of a kinsman to you, as Yahweh lives: lie down until the morning. **14** She lay at his feet until the morning. She rose up before one could discern another. For he said, Let it not be known that the woman came to the threshing floor. **15** He said, Bring the mantle that is on you, and hold it; and she held it; and he measured six [measures] of barley, and laid it on her: and he went into the city. **16** When she came to her mother-in-law, she said, Who are you, my daughter? She told her all that the man had done to her. **17** She said, These six [measures] of barley gave he me; for he said, "Don't go empty to your mother-in-law." **18** Then said she, "Sit still, my daughter, until you know how the matter will fall; for the man will not rest, until he has finished the thing this day."

Did you know?

God provided protection for widows in many different ways. You have already learned of one way; by providing food. Another way is through marriage. In Deuteronomy 25:5-10, God made a provision that if a woman is left without a husband and she has no children, that an un-married relative (for example a brother-in-law) may marry her. This would allow for him to take care of her.

Did you notice how well Ruth obeyed her mother-in-law in verse five? Do you think God wants you to obey your parents in the same way?

Chapter Four

1 Now Boaz went up to the gate, and sat him down there: and, behold, the near kinsman of whom Boaz spoke came by; to whom he said, Ho, such a one! turn aside, sit down here. He turned aside, and sat down. 2 He took ten men of the elders of the city, and said, Sit you down here. They sat down. 3 He said to the near kinsman, Naomi, who has come back out of the country of Moab, is selling the parcel of land, which was our brother Elimelech's: 4 I thought to disclose it to you, saying, Buy it before those who sit here, and before the elders of my people. If you will redeem it, redeem it: but if you will not redeem it, then

tell me, that I may know; for there is none to redeem it besides you; and I am after you. He said, I will redeem it. **5** Then said Boaz, What day you buy the field of the hand of Naomi, you must buy it also of Ruth the Moabitess, the wife of the dead, to raise up the name of the dead on his inheritance. **6** The near kinsman said, I can't redeem it for myself, lest I mar my own inheritance: take my right of redemption on you; for I can't redeem it. **7** Now this was [the custom] in former time in Israel concerning redeeming and concerning exchanging, to confirm all things: a man drew off his shoe, and gave it to his neighbor; and this was the [manner of] confirmation in Israel. **8** So the near kinsman said to Boaz, Buy it for yourself. He drew off his shoe. **9** Boaz said to the elders, and to all the people, You are witnesses this day, that I have bought all that was Elimelech's, and all that was Chilion's and Mahlon's, of the hand of Naomi. **10** Moreover Ruth the Moabitess, the wife of Mahlon, have I purchased to be my wife, to raise up the name of the dead on his inheritance, that the name of the dead not be cut off from among his brothers, and from the gate of his place: you are witnesses this day. **11** All the people who were in the gate, and the elders, said, We are witnesses. Yahweh make the woman who has come into your house like Rachel and like Leah, which two built the house of Israel: and do you worthily in Ephrathah, and be famous in Bethlehem: **12** and let your house be like the house of Perez, whom Tamar bore to Judah, of the seed which Yahweh shall give you of this young woman. **13** So Boaz took Ruth, and she became his wife; and he went in to her, and Yahweh gave her conception, and she bore a son. **14** The women said to Naomi, Blessed be Yahweh, who has not left you this day without a near kinsman; and let his name be famous in Israel. **15** He shall be to you a restorer of life, and sustain you in your old age, for your daughter-in-law, who loves you, who is better to you than seven sons, has borne him. **16** Naomi took the child, and laid it in her bosom, and became nurse to it. **17** The women her neighbors gave it a name, saying, There is a son born to Naomi; and they named him Obed: he is the father of Jesse, the father of David. **18** Now this is the history of the generations of Perez: Perez became the father of Hezron, **19** and Hezron became the father of Ram, and Ram became the father of Amminadab, **20** and Amminadab became the father of Nahshon, and Nahshon became the father of Salmon, **21** and Salmon became the father of Boaz, and Boaz became the father of Obed, **22** and Obed became the father of Jesse, and Jesse became the father of David.

Did you know?

Ruth, once a widow who had to gather scrapes of grain for Naomi and herself, now has become the wife of Boaz. She also has a son and the honor of being in the family line of King David, her great-grandson, and the King of King, Jesus Christ.

Can you see her obedience to God? In what ways did God fulfill His plan in Ruth's life?

The Book of Esther

Chapter One

1 Now it happened in the days of Ahasuerus (this is Ahasuerus who reigned from India even to Ethiopia, over one hundred twenty-seven provinces), **2** that in those days, when the king Ahasuerus sat on the throne of his kingdom, which was in Shushan the palace, **3** in the third year of his reign, he made a feast to all his princes and his servants; the power of Persia and Media, the nobles and princes of the provinces, being before him; **4** when he shown the riches of his glorious kingdom and the honor of his excellent majesty many days, even one hundred eighty days. **5** When these days were fulfilled, the king made a feast to all the people who were present in Shushan the palace, both great and small, seven days, in the court of the garden of the king's palace. **6** [There were hangings of] white [cloth], [of] green, and [of] blue, fastened with cords of fine linen and purple to silver rings and pillars of marble: the couches were of gold and silver, on a pavement of red, and white, and yellow, and black marble. **7** They gave them drink in vessels of gold (the vessels being diverse one from another), and royal wine in abundance, according to the bounty of the king. **8** The drinking was according to the law; none could compel: for so the king had appointed to all the officers of his house, that they should do according to every man's pleasure. **9** Also Vashti the queen made a feast for the women in the royal house which belonged to king Ahasuerus. **10** On the seventh day, when the heart of the king was merry with wine, he commanded Mehuman, Biztha, Harbona, Bigtha, and Abagtha, Zethar, and Carcass, the seven chamberlains who ministered in the presence of Ahasuerus the king, **11** to bring Vashti the queen before the king with the crown royal, to show the peoples and the princes her beauty; for she was beautiful to look on. **12** But the queen Vashti refused to come at the king's commandment by the chamberlains: therefore was the king very angry, and his anger burned in him. **13** Then the king said to the wise men, who knew the times, (for so was the king's manner toward all who knew law and judgment; **14** and the next to him were Carshena, Shethar, Admatha, Tarshish, Meres, Marsena, and Memucan, the seven princes of Persia and Media, who saw the king's face, and sat first in the kingdom), **15** What shall we do to the queen Vashti according to law, because she has not done the bidding of the king Ahasuerus by the chamberlains? **16** Memucan answered before the king and the princes, Vashti the queen has not done wrong to the king only, but also to all the princes, and to all the peoples who are in all the provinces of the king Ahasuerus. **17** For this deed of the queen will come abroad to all women, to make their husbands contemptible in their eyes, when it shall be reported, The king Ahasuerus commanded Vashti the queen to be brought in before him, but she didn't come. **18** This day will the princesses of Persia and Media who have heard of the deed of the queen say [the like] to all the king's princes. So [will there arise] much contempt and wrath. **19** If it please the king, let there go forth a royal commandment from him, and let it be written among the laws of the Persians and the Medes, that it not be altered, that Vashti come no more before king Ahasuerus; and let the king give her royal estate to another who is better than she. **20** When the king's decree which he shall make shall be published throughout all his kingdom (for it is great), all the wives will give to their husbands honor, both to great and small. **21** The saying pleased the king and the princes; and the king did according to the word of Memucan: **22** for he sent letters into all the king's provinces, into every province according to the writing of it, and to every people after their language, that every man should bear rule in his own house, and should speak according to the language of his people.

Did you know?

Any law that the King of Persia made could not be changed. For this reason, the king had to be very careful about which laws he created. Do you think King Ahasuerus thought through his decision to remove Queen Vashti? Have you ever made a choice you later regretted?

Before making a decision we should check to see that our choice is one that Jesus would make, "he who says he remains in him [Jesus] ought himself also to walk just like he walked" (1 John 2:6).

Chapter Two

1 After these things, when the wrath of king Ahasuerus was pacified, he remembered Vashti, and what she had done, and what was decreed against her. **2** Then said the king's servants who ministered to him, Let there be beautiful young virgins sought for the king: **3** and let the king appoint officers in all the provinces of his kingdom, that they may gather together all the beautiful young virgins to Shushan the palace, to the house of the women, to the custody of Hegai the king's chamberlain, keeper of the women; and let their things for purification be given them; **4** and let the maiden who pleases the king be queen instead of

Vashti. The thing pleased the king; and he did so. **5** There was a certain Jew in Shushan the palace, whose name was Mordecai, the son of Jair, the son of Shimei, the son of Kish, a Benjamite, **6** who had been carried away from Jerusalem with the captives who had been carried away with Jeconiah king of Judah, whom Nebuchadnezzar the king of Babylon had carried away. **7** He brought up Hadassah, who is, Esther, his uncle's daughter: for she had neither father nor mother, and the maiden was fair and beautiful; and when her father and mother were dead, Mordecai took her for his own daughter. **8** So it happened, when the king's commandment and his decree was heard, and when many maidens were gathered together to Shushan the palace, to the custody of Hegai, that Esther was taken into the king's house, to the custody of Hegai, keeper of the women. **9** The maiden pleased him, and she obtained kindness of him; and he speedily gave her things for her purification, with her portions, and the seven maidens who were meet to be given her out of the king's house: and he removed her and her maidens to the best place of the house of the women. **10** Esther had not made known her people nor her relatives; for Mordecai had charged her that she should not make it known. **11** Mordecai walked every day before the court of the women's house, to know how Esther did, and what would become of her. **12** Now when the turn of every maiden was come to go in to king Ahasuerus, after it had been done to her as prescribed for the women twelve months (for so were the days of their purification accomplished, [to wit], six months with oil of myrrh, and six months with sweet odors and with the things for the purifying of the women), **13** then in this wise came the maiden to the king: whatever she desired was given her to go with her out of the house of the women to the king's house. **14** In the evening she went, and on the next day she returned into the second house of the women, to the custody of Shaashgaz, the king's chamberlain, who kept the concubines: she came in to the king no more, except the king delighted in her, and she were called by name. **15** Now when the turn of Esther, the daughter of Abihail the uncle of Mordecai, who had taken her for his daughter, was come to go in to the king, she required nothing but what Hegai the king's chamberlain, the keeper of the women, appointed. Esther obtained favor in the sight of all those who looked at her. **16** So Esther was taken to king Ahasuerus into his house royal in the tenth month, which is the month Tebeth, in the seventh year of his reign. **17** The king loved Esther above all the women, and she obtained favor and kindness in his sight more than all the virgins; so that he set the royal crown on her head, and made her queen instead of Vashti. **18** Then the king made a great feast to all his princes and his servants, even Esther's feast; and he made a release to the provinces, and gave gifts, according to the bounty of the king. **19** When the virgins were gathered together the second time, then Mordecai was sitting in the king's gate. **20** Esther had not yet made known her relatives nor her people; as Mordecai had charged her: for Esther did the commandment of Mordecai, like as when she was brought up with him. **21** In those days, while Mordecai was sitting in the king's gate, two of the king's chamberlains, Bigthan and Teresh, of those who kept the threshold, were angry, and sought to lay hands on the king Ahasuerus. **22** The thing became known to Mordecai, who shown it to Esther the queen; and Esther told the king [of it] in Mordecai's name. **23** When inquisition was made of the matter, and it was found to be so, they were both hanged on a tree: and it was written in the book of the chronicles before the king.

Did you know?

The last sentence of verse 15 says, "Esther obtained favor in the sight of all those who looked at her." God, in His provenience, was in control of the situations around Esther so that she would be favored above all the other women and become queen.

God will use anyone He chooses to fulfill His plans. Esther was a young Jewish orphan and God made her queen of a nation.

Chapter Three

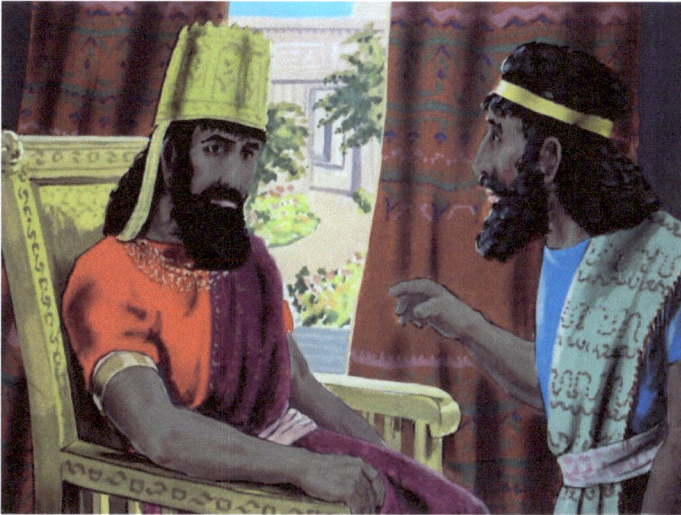

1 After these things did king Ahasuerus promote Haman the son of Hammedatha the Agagite, and advanced him, and set his seat above all the princes who were with him. **2** All the king's servants, who were in the king's gate, bowed down, and did reverence to Haman; for the king had so commanded concerning him. But Mordecai didn't bow down, nor did him reverence. **3** Then the king's servants, who were in the king's gate, said to Mordecai, Why disobey you the king's commandment? **4** Now it came to pass, when they spoke daily to him, and he didn't listen to them, that they told Haman, to see whether Mordecai's matters would stand: for he had told those who he was a Jew. **5** When Haman saw that Mordecai didn't bow down, nor did him reverence, then was Haman full of wrath. **6** But he thought scorn to lay hands on Mordecai alone; for they had made known to him the people of Mordecai: therefore Haman sought to destroy all the Jews who were throughout the whole kingdom of Ahasuerus, even the people of Mordecai. **7** In the first month, which is the month Nisan, in the twelfth year of king Ahasuerus, they cast Pur, that is, the lot, before Haman from day to day, and from month to month, [to] the twelfth [month], which is the month Adar. **8** Haman said to king Ahasuerus, There is a certain people scattered abroad and dispersed among the peoples in all the provinces of your kingdom; and their laws are diverse from [those of] every people; neither keep they the king's laws: therefore it is not for the king's profit to allow them. **9** If it please the king, let it be written that they be destroyed: and I will pay ten thousand talents of silver into the hands of those who have the charge of the [king's] business, to bring it into the king's treasuries. **10** The king took his ring from his hand, and gave it to Haman the son of Hammedatha the Agagite, the Jews' enemy. **11** The king said to Haman, The silver is given to you, the people also, to do with them as it seems good to you. **12** Then were the king's scribes called in the first month, on the thirteenth day of it; and there was written according to all that Haman commanded to the king's satraps, and to the governors who were over every province, and to the princes of every people, to every province according to the writing of it, and to every people after their language; in the name of king Ahasuerus was it written, and it was sealed with the king's ring. **13** Letters were sent by posts into all the king's provinces, to destroy, to kill, and to cause to perish, all Jews, both young and old, little children and women, in one day, even on the thirteenth [day] of the twelfth month, which is the month Adar, and to take the spoil of them for a prey. **14** A copy of the writing, that the decree should be given out in every province, was published to all the peoples, that they should be ready against that day. **15** The posts went forth in haste by the king's commandment, and the decree was given out in Shushan the palace. The king and Haman sat down to drink; but the city of Shushan was perplexed.

Did you know?

Haman became the second most powerful man in Persia. However, he was upset when Mordecai, Esther's older cousin who raised her as a father, would not bow to him. As a result Haman grew to hate Mordecai and all the Jews.

Jesus said that if you hate someone that God sees it as the same as murder (Mathew 5: 21-22). This is the sixth commandment and is called *murder of the heart*. Have you ever hated someone?

Chapter Four

1 Now when Mordecai knew all that was done, Mordecai tore his clothes, and put on sackcloth with ashes, and went out into the midst of the city, and cried with a loud and a bitter cry; **2** and he came even before the king's gate: for none might enter within the king's gate clothed with sackcloth. **3** In every province, wherever the king's commandment and his decree came, there was great mourning among the Jews, and fasting, and weeping, and wailing; and many lay in sackcloth and ashes. **4** Esther's maidens and her chamberlains came and told it her; and the queen was exceedingly grieved: and she sent clothing to clothe Mordecai, and to take his sackcloth from off him; but he didn't receive it. **5** Then called Esther for Hathach, one of the king's chamberlains, whom he had appointed to attend on her, and charged him to go to Mordecai, to know what this was, and why it was. **6** So Hathach went forth to Mordecai to the broad place of the city, which was before the king's gate. **7** Mordecai told him of all that had happened to him, and the exact sum of the money that Haman had promised to pay to the king's treasuries for the Jews, to destroy them. **8** Also he gave him the copy of the writing of the decree that was given out in Shushan to destroy them, to show it to Esther, and to declare it to her, and to charge her that she should go in to the king, to make supplication to him, and to make request before him, for her people. **9** Hathach came and told Esther the words of Mordecai. **10** Then Esther spoke to Hathach, and gave him a message to Mordecai [saying]: **11** All the king's servants, and the people of the king's provinces, do know, that whoever, whether man or woman, shall come to the king into the inner court, who is not called, there is one law for him, that he be put to death, except those to whom the king shall hold out the golden scepter, that he may live: but I have not been called to come in to the king these thirty days. **12** They told to Mordecai Esther's words. **13** Then Mordecai bade them return answer to Esther, Don't think to yourself that you shall escape in the king's house, more than all the Jews. **14** For if you altogether hold your peace at this time, then will relief and deliverance arise to the Jews from another place, but you and your father's house will perish: and who knows whether you haven't come to the kingdom for such a time as this? **15** Then Esther bade them return answer to Mordecai, **16** Go, gather together all the Jews who are present in Shushan, and fast you for me, and neither eat nor drink three days, night or day: I also and my maidens will fast in like manner; and so will I go in to the king, which is not according to the law: and if I perish, I perish. **17** So Mordecai went his way, and did according to all that Esther had commanded him.

Did you know?

To protect the king, no one could visit him unless they were invited. If they did so, they ran the risk of being punished to death. When Esther was asked by Mordecai to go in and see the king for the purpose of begging him to help the Jews, she was afraid that she would die. Nevertheless, she trusted God and left the results to him.

Have you ever been scared to do what you know is right? Esther asked others to pray for her so she would have the courage to obey. Maybe you should do the same.

Chapter Five

1 Now it happened on the third day, that Esther put on her royal clothing, and stood in the inner court of the king's house, over against the king's house: and the king sat on his royal throne in the royal house, over against the entrance of the house. **2** It was so, when the king saw Esther the queen standing in the court, that she obtained favor in his sight; and the king held out to Esther the golden scepter that was in his hand. So Esther drew near, and touched the top of the scepter. **3** Then said the king to her, What will you, queen Esther? and what is your request? it shall be given you even to the half of the kingdom. **4** Esther said, If it seem good to the king, let the king and Haman come this day to the banquet that I have prepared for him. **5** Then the king said, Cause Haman to make haste, that it may be done as Esther has said. So the king and Haman came to the banquet that Esther had prepared. **6** The king said to Esther at the banquet of wine, What is your petition? and it shall be granted you: and what is your request? even to the half of the kingdom it shall be performed. **7** Then answered Esther, and said, My petition and my request is: **8** if I have found favor in the sight of the king, and if it please the king to grant my petition, and to perform my request, let the king and Haman come to the banquet that I shall prepare for them, and I will do tomorrow as the king has said. **9** Then went Haman forth that day joyful and glad of heart: but when Haman saw Mordecai in the king's gate, that he didn't stand up nor move for him, he was filled with wrath against Mordecai. **10** Nevertheless Haman refrained himself, and went home; and he sent and fetched his friends and Zeresh his wife. **11** Haman recounted to them the glory of his riches, and the multitude of his children, and all the things in which the king had promoted him, and how he had advanced him above the princes and servants of the king. **12** Haman said moreover, Yes, Esther the queen did let no man come in with the king to the banquet that she had prepared but myself; and tomorrow also am I invited by her together with the king. **13** Yet all this avails me nothing, so long as I see Mordecai the Jew sitting at the king's gate. **14** Then said Zeresh his wife and all his friends to him, Let a gallows be made fifty cubits high, and in the morning speak you to the king that Mordecai may be hanged thereon: then go you in merrily with the king to the banquet. The thing pleased Haman; and he caused the gallows to be made.

Did you know?

Haman seemed to have everything. He wanted everyone to know it too. So he invited over his family and friends and bragged on himself. This is called pride.

God warned about being prideful. In Proverbs 16:18 God says, "Pride goes before destruction, A haughty [prideful] spirit before a fall." Is there something in your life that God deserves the credit for of which you have been bragging?

Chapter Six

1 On that night the king couldn't sleep; and he commanded to bring the book of records of the chronicles, and they were read before the king. **2** It was found written that Mordecai had told of Bigthana and Teresh, two of the king's chamberlains, of those who kept the threshold, who had sought to lay hands on the king Ahasuerus. **3** The king said, What honor and dignity has been bestowed on Mordecai for this? Then the king's servants who ministered to him said, "Nothing has been done for him." **4** The king said, "Who is in the court?" Now Haman was come into the outward court of the king's house, to speak to the king to hang

Mordecai on the gallows that he had prepared for him. **5** The king's servants said to him, Behold, Haman stands in the court. The king said, Let him come in. **6** So Haman came in. The king said to him, What shall be done to the man whom the king delights to honor? Now Haman said in his heart, To whom would the king delight to do honor more than to myself? **7** Haman said to the king, For the man whom the king delights to honor, **8** let royal clothing be brought which the king uses to wear, and the horse that the king rides on, and on the head of which a crown royal is set: **9** and let the clothing and the horse be delivered to the hand of one of the king's most noble princes, that they may array the man therewith whom the king delights to honor, and cause him to ride on horseback through the street of the city, and proclaim before him, Thus shall it be done to the man whom the king delights to honor. **10** Then the king said to Haman, Make haste, and take the clothing and the horse, as you have said, and do even so to Mordecai the Jew, who sits at the king's gate: let nothing fail of all that you have spoken. **11** Then took Haman the clothing and the horse, and arrayed Mordecai, and caused him to ride through the street of the city, and proclaimed before him, Thus shall it be done to the man whom the king delights to honor. **12** Mordecai came again to the king's gate. But Haman hurried to his house, mourning and having his head covered. **13** Haman recounted to Zeresh his wife and all his friends everything that had befallen him. Then said his wise men and Zeresh his wife to him, If Mordecai, before whom you have begun to fall, be of the seed of the Jews, you shall not prevail against him, but shall surely fall before him. **14** While they were yet talking with him, came the king's chamberlains, and hurried to bring Haman to the banquet that Esther had prepared.

Did you know?

It appears that the king did not know what Haman had been up to. The people of his kingdom must have been confused by his actions. One day he gives a decree that all the Jews shall be killed and then another gives the highest of honors publicly to a Jewish man.

We can see now that Haman's hatred towards the Jews and his pride has started to be his downfall. Even his wife and friends have begun to realize this.

Do you see how God has intervened for Esther in between her two banquets? In what ways has He done this?

Chapter Seven

1 So the king and Haman came to banquet with Esther the queen. **2** The king said again to Esther on the second day at the banquet of wine, What is your petition, queen Esther? and it shall be granted you: and what is your request? even to the half of the kingdom it shall be performed. **3** Then Esther the queen answered, If I have found favor in your sight, O king, and if it please the king, let my life be given me at my petition, and my people at my request: **4** for we are sold, I and my people, to be destroyed, to be slain, and to perish. But if we had been sold for bondservants and bondmaids, I had held my peace, although the adversary could not have compensated for the king's damage. **5** Then spoke the king Ahasuerus and said to Esther the queen, Who is he, and where is he, that dared presume in his heart to do so? **6** Esther said, An adversary and an enemy, even this wicked Haman. Then Haman was afraid before the king and the queen. **7** The king arose in his wrath from the banquet of wine [and went] into the palace garden: and Haman stood up to make request for his life to Esther the queen; for he saw that there was evil determined against him by the king. **8** Then the king returned out of the palace garden into the place of the banquet of wine; and Haman was fallen on the couch whereon Esther was. Then said the king, Will he even force the queen before me in the house? As the word went out of the king's mouth, they covered Haman's face. **9** Then said Harbonah, one of the chamberlains who were before the king, Behold also, the gallows fifty cubits high, which Haman has made for Mordecai, who spoke good for the king, stands in the house of Haman. The king said, Hang him thereon. **10** So they hanged Haman on the gallows that he had prepared for Mordecai. Then was the king's wrath pacified.

Did you know?

The king punished Haman as a murderer even though he had not completed his plans and had not killed a single Jewish person. This is because we are held accountable for our intentions and not just our actions. God looks at the heart, not just our actions. Are there bad things you have thought? God knows.

Chapter Eight

1 On that day did the king Ahasuerus give the house of Haman the Jews' enemy to Esther the queen. Mordecai came before the king; for Esther had told what he was to her. **2** The king took off his ring, which he had taken from Haman, and gave it to Mordecai. Esther set Mordecai over the house of Haman. **3** Esther spoke yet again before the king, and fell down at his feet, and begged him with tears to put away the mischief of Haman the Agagite, and his device that he had devised against the Jews. **4** Then the king held out to Esther the golden scepter. So Esther arose, and stood before the king. **5** She said, If it please the king, and if I have found favor in his sight, and the thing seem right before the king, and I be pleasing in his eyes, let it be written to reverse the letters devised by Haman, the son of Hammedatha the Agagite, which he wrote to destroy the Jews who are in all the king's provinces: **6** for how can I endure to see the evil that shall come to my people? or how can I endure to see the destruction of my relatives? **7** Then the king Ahasuerus said to Esther the queen and to Mordecai the Jew, See, I have given Esther the house of Haman, and him they have hanged on the gallows, because he laid his hand on the Jews. **8** Write you also to the Jews, as it pleases you, in the king's name, and seal it with the king's ring; for the writing which is written in the king's name, and sealed with the king's ring, may no man reverse. **9** Then were the king's scribes called at that time, in the third month Sivan, on the three and twentieth [day] of it; and it was written according to all that Mordecai commanded to the Jews, and to the satraps, and the governors and princes of the provinces which are from India to Ethiopia, one hundred twenty-seven provinces, to every province according to the writing of it, and to every people after their language, and to the Jews according to their writing, and according to their language. **10** He wrote the name of king Ahasuerus, and sealed it with the king's ring, and sent letters by post on horseback, riding on swift steeds that were used in the king's service, bred of the stud: **11** in which the king granted the Jews who were in every city to gather themselves together, and to stand for their life, to destroy, to kill, and to cause to perish, all the power of the people and province that would assault them, [their] little ones and women, and to take the spoil of them for a prey, **12** on one day in all the provinces of king Ahasuerus, [namely], on the thirteenth [day] of the twelfth month, which is the month Adar. **13** A copy of the writing, that the decree should be given out in every province, was published to all the peoples, and that the Jews should be ready against that day to avenge themselves on their enemies. **14** So the posts who rode on swift steeds that were used in the king's service went out, being hurried and pressed on by the king's commandment; and the decree was given out in Shushan the palace. **15** Mordecai went forth from the presence of the king in royal clothing of blue and white, and with a great crown of gold, and with a robe of fine linen and purple: and the city of Shushan shouted and was glad. **16** The Jews had light and gladness, and joy and honor. **17** In every province, and in every city, wherever the king's commandment and his decree came, the Jews had gladness and joy, a feast and a good day. Many from among the peoples of the land became Jews; for the fear of the Jews was fallen on them.

Did you know?

All that God does bring honor and glory to Himself. God also draws people to Him in order to save them and bring more glory to His name. We can see this in what happened when the King allowed the Jewish people to defend themselves. Look at what verse 17 says, "Many from among the peoples of the land became Jews."

What are some ways people could see that the God of the Jews was greater than the false Persian gods they worshiped?

Chapter Nine

1 Now in the twelfth month, which is the month Adar, on the thirteenth day of the same, when the king's commandment and his decree drew near to be put in execution, on the day that the enemies of the Jews hoped to have rule over them, (whereas it was turned to the contrary, that the Jews had rule over those who hated them,) 2 the Jews gathered themselves together in their cities throughout all the provinces of the king Ahasuerus, to lay hand on such as sought their hurt: and no man could withstand them; for the fear of them was fallen on all the peoples. 3 All the princes of the provinces, and the satraps, and the governors, and

those who did the king's business, helped the Jews; because the fear of Mordecai was fallen on them. 4 For Mordecai was great in the king's house, and his fame went forth throughout all the provinces; for the man Mordecai grew greater and greater. **5** The Jews struck all their enemies with the stroke of the sword, and with slaughter and destruction, and did what they would to those who hated them. **6** In Shushan the palace the Jews killed and destroyed five hundred men. **7** Parshandatha, and Dalphon, and Aspatha, **8** and Poratha, and Adalia, and Aridatha, **9** and Parmashta, and Arisai, and Aridai, and Vaizatha, **10** the ten sons of Haman the son of Hammedatha, the Jew's enemy, killed they; but they didn't lay their hand on the spoil. **11** On that day the number of those who were slain in Shushan the palace was brought before the king. **12** The king said to Esther the queen, The Jews have slain and destroyed five hundred men in Shushan the palace, and the ten sons of Haman; what then have they done in the rest of the king's provinces! Now what is your petition? and it shall be granted you: or what is your request further? and it shall be done. **13** Then said Esther, If it please the king, let it be granted to the Jews who are in Shushan to do tomorrow also according to this day's decree, and let Haman's ten sons be hanged on the gallows. **14** The king commanded it so to be done: and a decree was given out in Shushan; and they hanged Haman's ten sons. **15** The Jews who were in Shushan gathered themselves together on the fourteenth day also of the month Adar, and killed three hundred men in Shushan; but they didn't lay their hand on the spoil. **16** The other Jews who were in the king's provinces gathered themselves together, and stood for their lives, and had rest from their enemies, and killed of those who hated them seventy-five thousand; but they didn't lay their hand on the spoil. **17** [This was done] on the thirteenth day of the month Adar; and on the fourteenth day of the same they rested, and made it a day of feasting and gladness. **18** But the Jews who were in Shushan assembled together on the thirteenth [day] of it, and on the fourteenth of it; and on the fifteenth [day] of the same they rested, and made it a day of feasting and gladness. **19** Therefore do the Jews of the villages, who dwell in the unwalled towns, make the fourteenth day of the month Adar [a day of] gladness and feasting, and a good day, and of sending portions one to another. **20** Mordecai wrote these things, and sent letters to all the Jews who were in all the provinces of the king Ahasuerus, both near and far, **21** to enjoin those who they should keep the fourteenth day of the month Adar, and the fifteenth day of the same, yearly, **22** as the days in which the Jews had rest from their enemies, and the month which was turned to them from sorrow to gladness, and from mourning into a good day; that they should make them days of feasting and gladness, and of sending portions one to another, and gifts to the needy. **23** The Jews undertook to do as they had begun, and as Mordecai had written to them; **24** because Haman the son of Hammedatha, the Agagite, the enemy of all the Jews, had plotted against the Jews to destroy them, and had cast Pur, that is the lot, to consume them, and to destroy them; **25** but when [the matter] came before the king, he commanded by letters that his wicked device, which he had devised against the Jews, should return on his own head, and that he and his sons should be hanged on the gallows. **26** Therefore they called these days Purim, after the name of Pur. Therefore because of all the words of this letter, and of that which they had seen concerning this matter, and that which had come to them, **27** the Jews ordained, and took on them, and on their seed, and on all such as joined themselves to them, so that it should not fail, that they would keep these two days according to the writing of it, and according to the appointed time of it, every year; **28** and that these days should be remembered and kept throughout every generation, every family, every province, and every city; and that these days of Purim should not fail from among the Jews, nor the memory of them perish from their seed. **29** Then Esther the queen, the daughter of Abihail, and Mordecai the Jew, wrote with all authority to confirm this second letter of Purim. **30** He sent letters to all the Jews, to the hundred twenty-seven provinces of the kingdom of Ahasuerus, [with] words of peace and truth, **31** to confirm these days of Purim in their appointed times, according as Mordecai the Jew and Esther the queen had enjoined them, and as they had ordained for themselves and for their seed, in the matter of the fastings and their cry. **32** The commandment of Esther confirmed these matters of Purim; and it was written in the book.

Did you know?

God established a new holiday called Purim in this last chapter. This is the only place in the Bible this holiday is mentioned. Purim celebrates God's victory over the evil plot of Haman to destroy the Jewish people. It is celebrated in March by feasting, giving small gifts, and eating fruit-filled triangular cookies. During this celebration Esther is read aloud. When Haman's name is mentioned during this reading everyone makes a noise like hissing or stomping to blot it out.

Do you ever celebrate the things God has done for you?

Chapter Ten

1 The king Ahasuerus laid a tribute on the land, and on the isles of the sea. 2 All the acts of his power and of his might, and the full account of the greatness of Mordecai, whereunto the king advanced him, aren't they written in the book of the chronicles of the kings of Media and Persia? 3 For Mordecai the Jew was next to king Ahasuerus, and great among the Jews, and accepted of the multitude of his brothers, seeking the good of his people, and speaking peace to all his seed.

Did you know?

God raised Mordecai up to the highest level of government to provide protection for His people in Persia. God also did this before with Joseph in Egypt and Daniel in Babylon.

We can see how God is always in control even when we are threatened. Do you trust God when things seem to be going wrong? If not, try praying that God will give you comfort.

A Final Message

How do you know you are going to heaven? To find out we will start by asking a question. Do you consider yourself to be a good person? Most people think they are. This is because we have a different understanding of what "good" is from what the Bible says. We need to see what God says is good since He is the one in charge. Have you heard of the Ten Commandments? This is God's meaning of what "good" is. To be a good person to God you have to perfectly obey His commandments. Let's look at a couple of the commandments and see how you are doing.

The first commandment says, "You shall have no other gods before me." This means you should have loved God above everything else since the day you were born. Have you always loved God?

Another commandment, the third one, says you shall not take God's name in vain. This means you should have never used God name as a bad word. We can hear people breaking this commandment on TV all the time. Have you ever done that?

The fifth commandment says, "Honor your father and your mother." Have you always listened to your parents? This means giving them respect and obeying them even when it's not fun. If you kept this commandment it would mean you have always made your bed, came the first time your parents called, done your homework without fuss, and the list can go on.

In the sixth commandment God says, "You shall not murder." As we learned in the story of Esther, God sees hate as murder. Jesus said that if you even call someone a fool you have broken this one.

What about lying? The ninth commandment says you shouldn't tell lies. Have you ever lied or cheated? In fact, if you have ever lied to your parents you have broken this commandment and the fifth commandment at the same time.

So how are you doing? Did you know that God's law is perfect and He command you to be perfect? In Mathew 5:48 Jesus said, "Therefore you shall be perfect, just as your Father in heaven is perfect." He is going to punish everyone who is not perfect and has broken His law; liars, thieves, murders, and so on. He will even judge your words and thoughts. So on Judgment Day, do you think God will find you innocent or guilty of breaking his commandments?

Does it concern you that if you died today God would find you guilty and punish you? The Bible says that punishment is to be sent to Hell forever.

God doesn't want you to go to Hell. Do you know what God did so you don't have to go there? He provided a substitute for you as Jesus Christ. God Himself came down and He died on the cross to take the punishment you deserve for all your lying, stealing, hatred, and disobedience.

But this does not mean everyone goes to heaven. The Bible says you must repent and put your trust in Jesus. Do you know what repent means? Repent means that first, you agree with God that you have broken His laws and deserve punishment, and then you turn away from those bad things you have been doing and turn to God and do what He says. Then you put your trust in Jesus to save you, just like you put your trust in your parents to provide you food, clothes and a place to live. So confess your sins (the bad things you have done.) to God right now and put your trust in Him to save you from Hell. Then read your Bible everyday and obey it.